Jackson Pollock: Psychoanalytic Drawings

Jackson Pollock: Psychoanalytic Drawings

text by **C. L. Wysuph**

Horizon Press *New York*

Drawings © 1970 by Fred Maxwell
Text © 1970 by C. L. Wysuph
Library of Congress Catalog Card No. 72-132329
ISBN 0-8180-0115-1 (cloth), 0-8180-0116-x (paper)
Printed in the United States of America

To Fred Maxwell

Contents

There is no excellent beauty that hath not some strangeness in the proportio[n]

—Francis Baco[n]

Before art, psychoanalysis lays down its arm[s]

—Sigmund Freu[d]

I

Even before his untimely death in August, 1956, Jackson Pollock had become an almost legendary figure in American art. Since his death the legend has been so amplified and distorted that at times it is difficult to distinguish the man from the myth.[1]

The critical literature about the artist and his life ranges from Clement Greenberg's early reviews[2] to Francis O'Connor's biographical chronology[3] and includes such diverse writing as Michael McClure's "Ode to Jackson Pollock"[4] and a recent suggestion that Pollock's life and art be seen "as a space-time continuum."[5]

Implicit in most discussions of Pollock and his art is an assumption that the eccentricities of his personality, his extreme emotional states, are more evident in his work than is true in the case of other artists. We are often told that Pollock was a "disturbed," a "tormented" man, capable of physical violence as well as of verbal assaults on friends and enemies alike. His alcoholism has also been publicized, as has the notion that he worked in a "trance," a notion supported by his own statements about being "in the painting," the "arena" which had "a life of its own" and which sprang from the "unconscious."

Occasionally, however, we glimpse another man whose fundamentally gentle nature is complemented by unusual acumen. Such apparent duality might characterize many alcoholics, but Pollock was subject to sudden, radical changes of mood and temper even when he was not drinking. Lee Krasner Pollock has described him thus: "Whatever Jack-

[1]See Thomas B. Hess, "Pollock: The Art of a Myth," *Art News,* LXII, Jan. 1964.

[2]See especially the early reviews in *The Nation,* Nov. 27, 1943, p. 621; April 7, 1945, p. 397; April 13, 1946; p. 445; Dec. 28, 1946, p. 768; Feb. 1, 1947, pp.137-139; Jan. 24, 1948, p. 108; Feb. 19, 1949; p. 221; see also "The Present Prospects of American Painting and Sculpture," *Horizon* (London), No. 93-94, Oct. 1947, pp. 20-30.

[3]*Jackson Pollock,* The Museum of Modern Art, New York, 1967. See also O'Connor, "Growth Out of Need," *Report,* I, Feb. 1964, pp. 27-28; "The Genesis of Jackson Pollock: 1912-1943," *Artforum*, V, May, 1967, pp. 16-23.

[4]In *Evergreen Review,* II, Autumn, 1958, pp. 124-126.

[5]Tomassoni, Italo, *Pollock,* Grosset and Dunlap, New York, 1968, p. 9.

son felt, he felt more intensely than anyone I've known; when he was angry, he was angrier; when he was happy, he was happier; when he was quiet, he was quieter…'' A man, then, of extreme complexity, of extreme intensity: a man of extremes.

Almost all the critics who have written about Pollock make some allusions to his illness, and to the influence of Jungian psychology and therapy on his art; yet they have made no attempts to assess the effects of his illness on his creative decisions. Some consideration of his medical history in relation to the drawings reproduced here is in order.

By January 1939, Pollock's condition was critical. Though he had entered psychotherapy previously, he now sought help from a Jungian psychiatrist, Dr. Joseph Henderson. Initially withdrawn and inarticulate, Pollock was unable to discuss his problems openly. When he tried to talk about himself, he would do so in an impersonal manner, and then only refer to the most superficial aspects of his life. Finally, in an effort to open communication and perhaps recalling earlier psychotherapeutic experiments, he began to make drawings to supplement words where words alone had been inadequate. With his drawings as a reference, Pollock was able to discuss his emotional difficulties with considerably less reserve. Over the next 18 months he submitted to Henderson 69 sheets of drawings (13 of which contained drawings on both sides) and one gouache painting, in order, according to Henderson, to illustrate ''the experience he had been through. They seemed to demonstrate phases of his sickness …showing a gradual psychological reintegration which allowed him to recover to a considerable extent during the next two years.''[6]

When in 1940 Henderson left New York to set up practice in San Francisco, these drawings were the only record of his encounter with a young man who was to become a major American artist. They remained in Henderson's possession for almost 30 years until, in 1969, they were acquired by Fred Maxwell, President of Maxwell Galleries in San Francisco.[7]

[6]Joseph Henderson, M.D., ''Jackson Pollock: A Psychological Commentary.'' Unpublished essay.

[7]Maxwell acquired 67 sheets of drawings and one signed gouache. Dr. Henderson reports that the two sheets he kept are not, psychologically, of any particular interest and that their selection was a matter of personal taste.

Except for two drawings reproduced in 1967 by The Museum of Modern Art,[8] they have never been published before.

The nature and extent of the change in Pollock's style, a change which coincides with his work with Dr. Henderson, suggest that it cannot be accounted for adequately by stylistic analysis alone. I should like to offer some thoughts on the relation between psychotherapeutic needs and the metamorphosis of style.

II

Paul Jackson Pollock was the youngest of five sons born to Stella May McClure and LeRoy Pollock. He was born in Cody, Wyoming, on January 28, 1912. His father, a farmer, appears to have been a quiet, mild-mannered man "who left little mark on life and was defeated by the Depression."[9] His mother, on the other hand, was a woman of strong character who exercised the real force within the family. Information about Stella Pollock is provided mainly by Jackson's biographers. Bryan Robertson describes her as fitting "almost too conveniently into the popular notion of American matriarchy," and Francis O'Connor describes her thus:

> Stella was strong-willed and alert to opportunities. Her oldest son Charles recalls her as the impetus behind the family's many new starts [they moved nine times between 1912 and 1928]...she was certainly the dominant force in the family. Her ambitions were her sons. It is said she at times wished to have been an artist. In any event her five sons...sought out the life of art.[10]

By 1922 the members of the family began to separate, and by 1926 only Jackson and his brother Sanford (three years his elder) remained with their parents.

[8]Op. cit. O'Connor, *Jackson Pollock,* p. 85.

[9]Robertson, Bryan, *Jackson Pollock,* Abrams, New York, 1960, p. 88.

[10]Op. cit. O'Connor. "The Genesis of Jackson Pollock," p. 16.

Partly because of their frequent moves, Pollock made few friends outside his family. He was a quiet, inarticulate boy, and the only characteristic which we can attribute to him with any assurance is a tendency to periods of depression and withdrawal.

At 16, Pollock enrolled in Manual Arts High School in Los Angeles, and before the year's end was expelled for having taken part in the publishing and distribution of two broadsides attacking the faculty and the school's over-emphasis on sports. He returned to the school in 1929, but within the first month was in trouble again with the Physical Education department. From his letters, we learn that Jackson had come "to blows" with the head of the department, had attended Communist Party meetings during his expulsion, had showed an interest in Oriental philosophy, and had stated that people "frightened and bored" him. It is not surprising that such a boy should reveal—with his older brother's encouragement—an interest, even a commitment to being an artist.

Pollock left high school and, in September of 1930, enrolled in Thomas Hart Benton's class at the Art Student's League in New York. During the next few years it became obvious to those who were close to him that Pollock was suffering from serious emotional difficulties. In 1934 Pollock, who was working as a janitor at the City and Country School, was befriended by Caroline Pratt, the school's director, and Helen Marot, a teacher there. O'Connor reports that "both women took an interest in the troubled young man and were to be sources of encouragement and help to him throughout the thirties." This was especially true of Helen Marot, who was deeply interested in Jungian psychology and who was to remain a close friend to Pollock until her death in 1940.

Between 1934 and 1937, Pollock's emotional condition seems to have progressively deteriorated, and in 1937 he underwent about eight months of psychiatric treatment for acute alcoholism. The type of treatment he received is not clear.[11] In a letter of July, 1937, Pollock's brother Sanford wrote:

Jack has been having a very difficult time with himself. This

[11]Pollock's psychiatrist may have utilized art therapy. In any case it was Pollock who suggested that he use drawings as an aid to discussing himself with Henderson in 1939.

past year has been a succession of periods of emotional instability for him, which is usually expressed by a complete loss of responsibility both to himself and us. Accompanied, of course, with drinking. It came to the point where it was obvious that the man needed help. He was mentally sick. So I took him to a well recommended Doctor, a Psychiatrist, who has been trying to help the man find himself. As you know troubles such as his are very deep-rooted, in childhood usually, and it takes a long while to get them ironed out. He has been going some six months now and I feel there is a slight improvement in his point of view. So without giving the impression that I am trying to be a wet nurse to Jack, honestly, I would be fearful of the results if he were left alone with no one to keep him in check...There is no cause for alarm, he simply must be watched and guided intelligently.

Sanford's concern was apparently justified by the unsuccessful results of Jackson's treatment. In February 1938, he indicated in another letter that during the winter Jackson had been "in serious mental shape." In June, Jackson was hospitalized, at his own request, at the Westchester Division of New York Hospital for treatment of acute alcoholism; he remained until September. Soon after his release he suffered another relapse and, early in 1939, was referred for treatment by Mrs. Cary Baynes, through his friend Helen Marot, to Dr. Henderson, a Jungian psychoanalyst.

Dr. Henderson, who was then in his first year of practice, kept no notes about the sessions; aside from a professional interest, he was not particularly responsive to Pollock as an artist. To Henderson, his patient was an unknown artist suffering from a serious mental disturbance.

The extent to which Dr. Henderson may have entered into detailed analytic discussions of the drawings with Pollock is not clear. Dr. Henderson recalls only that he indicated to Pollock those characteristics in his work which seemed to represent "healthy" or "unhealthy" signs. In an unpublished paper on Pollock, however, he reflects thus on his therapeutic method:

I wonder why I neglected to find out, study or analyze his personal problems in the first year of his work...I wonder why I did not seem to try to cure his alcoholism...I have decided that it is because his unconscious drawings brought me strongly into a state of counter-transference to the symbolic material he produced. Thus I was compelled to follow the movement of his symbolism as inevitably as he was motivated to produce it.

During the first year of Pollock's work with Henderson, attention seems to have been focussed almost exclusively on the drawings. Apparently Pollock was convinced that his psychological difficulties were revealed in imagery. While his imagery was obviously conditioned by and often drawn from the work of Surrealist artists, it retained an autonomous character which responded to needs much more basic than the mere adaptation of Surrealist iconography. Indeed the causes of Pollock's response to Surrealism and to psychic automatism are to be found in the nature and effect of his mental crisis of 1938-1940, and particularly in Henderson's emphasis on the psychological relevance of visual symbols. Therefore it will be instructive to summarize Henderson's commentary on the nature of Pollock's illness and its reflection in his drawing.

Henderson diagnosed Pollock's illness as schizophrenia, indicated by periods of "violent agitation"; by states of "paralysis or withdrawal"; and by "a pathological form of introversion."

During periods of "violent agitation" Pollock seemed incapable of rendering clearly articulated shapes, and produced impulsive, jagged drawings (nos. 2 and 3).

"Withdrawal" was indicated by Pollock's turning his attention inward until he dissociated himself completely from the world around him. Sanford Pollock's wife Arloie recalls that Pollock, who was living with his brother's family, would become unusually quiet and depressed for a few days before going on a "binge." The binge would in turn be followed by a period of solitude and depression. Then, sober, Pollock would begin a period of intense painting and drawing. Lee Krasner has noted that this pattern continued into the late '40's and that during periods of depression Jackson "would become so withdrawn as to be impenetrable."

Henderson refers to drawing no. 64 as representative of Pollock's state of withdrawal. Here the eyes of an apathetic world watch a primitive ritual sacrifice in which a woman defends herself and a child against men who would offer them to what appears to be a bird-monster at an altar. To Dr. Henderson the grotesque nature of this scene suggested Pollock's fear of psychic disability and withdrawal (scenes of sacrifice recur in many drawings, as do bird images). Drawing no. 16 also represents for Henderson Pollock's state of withdrawal. Here a thin white line surrounds an agitated rendering of confused human and animal forms. Withdrawal is also indicated by a claustrophobic compaction of forms within a specified area and by ambiguity of line—that is, lines and shapes serving several functions. These tendencies are said to be characteristic of schizophrenic art in general,[12] and are closely related to the third symptom of Henderson's diagnosis, a pathological form of introversion.

Introversion is represented in drawing no. 10, about which Henderson wrote:

> All energy seems to have been drawn from the upper "conscious" region, which appears lifeless, wooden and anguished. The life force or psychic energy is represented by the huge snake (lower center) which denotes the unconscious and upon which the human figure is completely and dependently attached.

According to Henderson, Pollock's art began to develop "healthier" signs during the period of their association. Although Pollock's problems were never resolved—indeed they seem to have grown progressively worse— he was able to sustain a high degree of productivity for the next few years.

[12]See Ernst Kris, *Psychological Explorations in Art,* International Universities Press, New York, 1952, pp. 94 ff. Kris notes that schizophrenic art is characterized by "configurations which bear the imprint of the primary process [and] tend to be ambiguous, allowing for more than one interpretation." Kris also refers to a concurrent tendency of schizophrenics to "fill the borders" in a kind of *"horror vacui."* Obviously this does not mean that all art sharing these characteristics is schizophrenic; "under certain conditions even those traits in artistic creation which are linked to what we can clinically describe as pathological processes may actually enhance the effect. This may happen especially when for certain historical reasons the very emphasis on conflict, or some obvious contrast which we may clinically attribute to the upsurge of Id impulses and the defense against them, gains high social approval."

While the crucifixion in drawing no. 1 suggested to Henderson self-punishment and perhaps death, the stabilizing effect of the cross and the red spot (sun?) represented a new conscious ordering of elements. In this context he felt that Pollock was acting out a symbolic dismemberment which would be followed by new growth and mature ego control:

> The patient appears to have been in a state similar to the novice in a tribal initiation rite during which he is ritually dismembered at the onset of an ordeal whose goal is to change him from a boy to a man.

Similarly the mandaloid form of drawing no. 30 represented for Henderson a new symbol-ordering influence; especially in symbols of complex male-female unions indicated by the presence of crossed arrows and primitive embryonic forms.[13]

In drawing no. 36 Henderson was encouraged by the presence of a half-formed skeletal figure and a small mandala (lower center). The vertical design—representing a dead human coming back to life in accordance with the snake-like movement of the vertebrae—again suggested psychic stability through vertical growth and symbol control.

The most significant example of symbolical growth is represented by drawing no. 57, about which Henderson wrote:

> The oval-shaped area in the center with its plant symbol suggests that the principle of psychic growth or development is the central meaning of the pole which is therefore not only a sexual symbol (if at all) but represents the primitive conception of the *axis mundi* which stands for the strength of tribal identity and by analogy is the new ego-strength the patient is hoping to attain.

---

[13]For an interesting though brief discussion of a general tendency toward biomorphism, see Lawrence Alloway, "The Biomorphic Forties," *Artforum*, VI, No. 1, Sept. 1965. Alloway discusses a tradition of biomorphism as a vehicle of the unconscious: "Proliferating biomorphism is the analogue of manic activity in the artist . . . Pollock in drawings of the late '30's made what are virtually straight biomorphic exercises. These chain-reactions of repetitive and transforming imagery are presumably the type of drawing that he discussed with his Jungian analyst in 1939."

But Henderson finds other, less encouraging elements in this drawing:

> ...the upper part of the drawing shows a continuing split and
> a probable state of deprivation on the upper, human per-
> sonal level of his life. Those pathetic upper limbs reaching
> upward toward an unfeeling, purely schematic, female torso
> must denote a problem left unsolved and perhaps insoluble,
> a frustrated longing for the all-giving mother. He had suf-
> fered from isolation and extreme emotional deprivation in
> early childhood and this had not yet been adequately com-
> pensated. We can only conjecture whether this need was
> satisfied in his later marriage and personal relationships.

Pollock's "frustrated longing for the all-giving mother" is also reflected in drawing no. 58, in which a prominent female figure appears to be deny-ing a child access to her breast; her hand is raised as if to strike the in-fant's already dislocated head, and the suggestion of violent encounter is intensified by the jagged teeth she bares against his approach.

In this regard, Henderson suggests that the women so frequent in Pollock's iconography may represent aspects of his need for "the all-giving mother." Henderson is also convinced that Pollock's mother was central to his difficulties.

At this period, three people came to play an especially important role in Pollock's life: Helen Marot, on whose counsel and friendship he relied extensively; his brother Sanford, who had been one of his closest personal contacts; and Dr. Henderson, whose help permitted Pollock to relieve the intense anxieties from which he suffered.

Helen Marot became, in Henderson's words, a "substitute mother figure" upon whom Pollock relied "for his need to give and receive feel-ing." Her sudden death early in 1940 must have been a blow to Pollock. The psychiatrist supplied the needed "substitute father figure" upon whom Jackson relied mainly "to help structure his thinking function to-ward achieving a more rational and objective view of his life and art"; while his brother Sanford "carried much of his reality function."

Soon after Helen Marot's death, Henderson left New York for San Francisco. The effect on Pollock of the dispersal of this trio must have been profound. On the other hand, Henderson asserts that some progress had been made and that his and Miss Marot's continued presence might have served only to prolong his patient's dependence on them.

Although Pollock was referred to another analyst with whom he worked for the next few years, he insisted on the primary importance of his experience with Henderson. He continued, Lee Krasner Pollock remembered, to refer to it in terms which suggest its profound impact on his life. Three months before his death, he said, "I've been a Jungian for a long time."[14]

During this period Pollock's art was changing radically. He may have experimented with free-association drawing as early as 1937, but he did not begin to produce "abstract" work until after his release from New York Hospital. Sanford recalls that it was then that Jackson's art "went for the first time abstract."[15] In May, 1940, Sanford wrote to Charles:

> Jack is doing very good work. After years of trying to work along lines completely unsympathetic to his nature, he has finally dropped the Benton nonsense and is coming out with an honest creative art.

Sanford's recollection that Pollock first turned to abstract art after his release from New York Hospital and his letter indicating that Jackson had "finally dropped the Benton nonsense" in mid-1940 raises some questions concerning the dating of many of Pollock's works before 1939. Certainly Jackson's hospitalization represented a landmark event for Sanford, more easily remembered than specific dates. Regardless of these uncertainties, or rather because of them, Francis O'Connor has distinguished two chief periods in Pollock's early development. The first extends from the time he entered the League until his mental crisis of 1938; the second from then until his first show at the Art of This Century

[14]From an interview between Selden Rodman and Jackson Pollock, June 1956, published in *Conversations with Artists,* Devin-Adair, New York, 1957, p. 82.

[15]From an interview between Sanford McCoy (Pollock) and Clement Greenberg, 1956, in O'Connor, "The Genesis of Jackson Pollock."

Gallery. The first period was characterized by strong influences from Benton and, later, Rivera and Ryder. The second period by influences from Surrealism and psychic automatism.[16]

But the dramatic change in Pollock's style between 1938 and 1940 was too radical, too complete to be accounted for solely by references to models and influences from within the art world. Working with Henderson, Pollock had become more keenly aware of the psychological relevance of visual symbols and was forced to adopt a new esthetic vocabulary with which to articulate a new need. O'Connor suggests as much in the last footnote to his article:

> The radical change in Pollock's art at this time...reflecting as it does the influences of Surrealism and psychic automatism—must be seen in conjunction with the fact that in about 1940-41 [O'Connor corrected these dates later] Pollock was undergoing Jungian analysis. His whole personality was undergoing a radical change...To my mind Surrealism is for Pollock at this time not so much an overt artistic influence as a subtle permission to be creatively free.

O'Connor apparently recognized that stylistic affinities with the Surrealists were not sufficient to account for Pollock's sudden departure from his own style as it had developed up to 1938, and that Surrealism—never fully accommodated in Pollock's art—was only the vehicle of another, deeper influence.

III

According to Henderson, Pollock was already familiar at the time with the Surrealist notion of psychic automatism and acquainted as well with the principles of Jungian psychology. Rather than the overt political and social statements of Benton, Siquieros and Rivera, he must have felt

[16]*Op. cit.,* O'Connor, "The Genesis of Jackson Pollock."

the need to express a more interior reality. Pollock's breakdown made the need an imperative: to turn away from man in general to Jackson Pollock in particular. His abrupt turn to Surrealist imagery is thus consistent with his need for a new symbolic vocabulary with which to articulate the unconscious.

From 1940 on, there is a continuous and consistent metamorphosis of style in Pollock's work, a transformation which persists through 1950. The new style was a development of three fundamental characteristics: all-over drawing; automatic drawing to elicit unconscious imagery; obscuring or veiling this imagery.

All-over drawing, a characteristic of many of the drawings, means a dense compaction of shapes within a specified border (not necessarily the edges of the paper), giving the impression that all available space has been filled.

Part of the mysterious quality of Pollock's later paintings is the presence of obscure images lurking in the shallow webs of over-painting. This effect was the result of working ''from the inside out''—that is, of striking out images which formed the original composition. As William Rubin puts it:

> As we study these key transitional works [*Shimmering Substance* and *Eyes in the Heat*], we become aware that fragments of Pollock's earlier totemic presences are *covered* by the rhythmical linear patterns of white paint...these presences have not been wholly ''painted out'' but lurk mysteriously in the interstices of the white lines . . .[17]

In Pollock's work, this method of abstraction began as a process in which images were distorted and eventually dissolved in a plethora of lines. In drawing no. 49, for example, human and animal elements are so interwoven that neither is dominant. Images are fused until in the upper portion they are almost indistinguishable; and in the lower portion, the opposing direction of legs anticipates the diffusion of solid masses occurring

[17]William Rubin, ''Jackson Pollock and the Modern Tradition, Part I'' *Artforum*, V, No. 6, Feb. 1967, p. 15.

in the upper half. The inter-relationship of dissimilar and opposing elements creates visual tension as plasticity gives way to fluidity and non-representational abstraction.

The initial form is even more abstracted in drawing no. 9, one of the few for which a preliminary study may be found. This drawing may have originated in a Picassoid sketch in drawing no. 8 (lower center). The human figure in no. 8 is completely lost in no. 9, and only suggestions of the horse, the general composition, colors and relative positioning of the feet are retained. Like his later paintings, this drawing suggests only the "presence" of an original image, the formal shape of which has been veiled by many linear derivations. The solid form is dissolved in the interweaving lines. In both no. 49 and no. 9, Pollock engaged in a process of abstraction which would eventually lead to the total destruction of overt imagery.

Another example of this process occurs in drawings no. 24 and 25; the images of no. 24, recalling Picasso, provide only the rudiments of composition in no. 25. In no. 24, a head (lower left), a horse's neck and head (upper left), and the "V" configuration of the lower part become in no. 25 an arm, hand and double knee, respectively. What is important here is that the figure in no. 25 is itself in process of dissolution. This ambiguous, half-clear figure is becoming one of the "presences" of which Rubin spoke.[18]

Drawing no. 2 reflects that propensity more clearly; only hints of identifiable objects such as fish, eyes, an emerging arm, are given. In this regard the drawing is a formative idea leading eventually to such works as *Eyes in the Heat.* Such "presences" appear or are felt in many other drawings of this series.

The apparent contradiction in Pollock's desire to create and simultaneously to destroy imagery may be consistent with Henderson's belief that a psychic birth-death-rebirth cycle was essential to the maintenance of Pollock's sanity. In any case, his reluctance to discuss himself or his art suggests an analogous reluctance to *expose* his imagery which, he was convinced, revealed his innermost struggles, the most personal and perhaps most painful aspects of his life. Just as he avoided talking about

[18]*Ibid.*

himself, he sought by camouflaging his imagery to disguise even inadvertent self-revelation.

In 1945, Lee Krasner Pollock discussed with Jackson a painting then in progress *(There Were Seven in Eight)*. When she asked why he would not leave it in its present state, Pollock said, "I choose to veil the image." Surely, as a result of his association with Henderson as well as of his own study, he could read the signs of his precarious state of mind in his own imagery. He said, "I'm a little representational all of the time. But when you're painting out of your unconscious, figures are bound to emerge."[19] It is clear that Pollock associated the unconscious with figures, not with non-representational overpainting. If figures revealed his illness, would it not be an affirmation of positive control to hide or obliterate what had been unconsciously created? His veils, like his drip paintings, were technically too refined, too sophisticated, too "academic" to represent the unconscious aspect of his art.

Rubin has said that the aim of Pollock's drip method

> was to circumvent the operation of those pictorial inhibitions which derive from habit, expectations and immersions in a tradition and to reach…through automatism, into areas of unconscious experience which might not otherwise be tapped.[20]

And Harold Rosenberg has defined Action Painting as follows:

> If the ultimate subject matter of all art is the artist's psychic state…that state may be represented either through the image of a thing or through an abstract sign. The innovation of Action Painting was to dispense with the *representation* of the state in favor of *enacting* it in physical movement. The action on the canvas became its own representation.[21]

[19]*Op. cit.* Rodman, *Conversations with Artists,* p. 82.

[20]*Op. cit.* Rubin, p. 15.

[21]Harold Rosenberg, "Hans Hofmann; Nature into Action," *Art News,* May, 1957. Reprinted in *The Anxious Object,* Horizon Press, New York, 1964, p. 155.

Both these statements articulate not the *cause* of Pollock's art but its *effect,* the effect of his method. If the aim of Pollock's drip method was not to "reach...into areas of unconscious experiences" but to veil those unconscious experiences which had already been tapped in the preliminary process of eliciting automatic imagery, then the second stage of his painting—the one he reveals to us—is not the "automatic" stage but rather the "academic" stage. In fact this second stage is the more controlled of the two, since its ultimate character is prescribed by an underlying figurative motive. This hypothesis would seem untenable with regard to Pollock's exclusively drip period of 1948-1950, were it not for the fact that Pollock considered even these works as figurative in concept. As Mrs. Pollock has said, these paintings are "no less figurative" than his earlier work, but the figures and the "veils" are so integrated as to be indistinguishable. If this is true, then Pollock's method answered two needs, personal and esthetic: to act out an internal struggle, and to conceal it; to articulate an identity, and to prevent access to the person.

IV

One paradox of Pollock's art centers around the apparent absence of demonstrable antecedents. Thus we have Allan Kaprow writing as follows:

> Pollock really misused his sources by all conventional standards, taking from them rather marginal attributes or tones of feeling rather than developing their central principles. Pollock may be the first major artist who, after a pathetic apprenticeship to older art, was able to become major by ignoring demonstrable familiarity with existing models.[22]

As we have seen, this may be due to Pollock's method of abstraction, in which few or none of the original motifs are retained. As a result, his style appears to be a spontaneous invention—without precursors, unexpected, unique.

[22]Allan Kaprow, "Jackson Pollock: An Artists' Symposium, Part I," *Art News,* April 1967, p. 60.

In an effort to identify the origins of Pollock's esthetic, some critics suggested, even before his death, that the ultimate sources of his inspiration could somehow be traced to his experiences in the American west; the expanse of the Grand Canyon, Indian sand painting and textile decoration. Obviously the total experience of a man's life makes up his personality, and to that extent these possibilities may have been operative. Although Pollock likened his method to that of the Indian sand painter, he denied any reference to the motifs of Indian art.[23] I am inclined to think that these primitivist analogies were so remote from the immediacy of Pollock's work as to be negligible. Whatever "primitive" concepts are to be found in his work probably came second-hand, through Picasso, Surrealism and Jungian psychology.

Related to the notion that Pollock's inspiration stems from a "western" experience is Frank O'Hara's assertion that some of Pollock's early paintings developed out of his interest in certain myths. While it is true that his titles often suggest mythological origins—he was doubtless influenced by Jungian references to mythology—I find untenable O'Hara's theory that the myth of Romulus and Remus underlies *The She-Wolf, Bird Effort, Wounded Animal, Guardian of the Secret, Male and Female,* and *There Were Seven in Eight.* The credibility of O'Hara's theory depends on his interpretation of *The She-Wolf:*

> In *The She-Wolf*...one of the six works which bear on the probability of allegory, Lupa, the saving nurse of Romulus and Remus, is advancing with full dugs toward a child whose face appears in the lower left. This is undoubtedly Romulus, for though the wolf nursed both brothers, Romulus later killed Remus. She is not yet giving suck, and Romulus, the stronger, would be the first to feed.[24]

[23]Jackson Pollock, "My Painting," *Possibilities I,* Winter 1947-48. "On the floor I am more at ease. I feel nearer, more a part of the painting, since this way I can walk round it, work from the four sides and literally be *in* the painting. This is akin to the method of the Indian sand painters of the West." "Answers to a Questionnaire," *Arts and Architecture,* LXI, Feb. 1944, p. 14. "Some people find references to American Indian art and calligraphy in parts of my pictures. That wasn't intentional . . ." The answers to this questionnaire were prepared by Pollock with the assistance of Howard Putzel.

[24]O'Hara, Frank, *Jackson Pollock,* George Braziller, Inc., New York, 1959, p. 18.

A "wolf" motif rarely if ever appears in Pollock's drawings, and to my knowledge never again in his painting (except perhaps in *Wounded Animal).* On the other hand, horses, bulls and cows occur with great frequency. We should not be surprised then to find that *The She-Wolf* is not a wolf at all, or if she is, a curious breed with squared nose, horns, humped back, hoofed feet, udders and a short-haired tail.

Pollock's titles are often cryptic and sometimes misleading. Mrs. Pollock observes that though the artist was very serious about them, he seldom if ever explained his titles. Was this title another form of veil, or was it in fact related to the myth of Romulus? It seems that when Pollock titled his paintings, the title reflected his interpretation of it *after the fact.* That is, he would produce a painting "out of the unconscious" and then read it, and from the reading derive a title; but by the time the underlying motifs had been veiled, the title reflected not what we are permitted to see but what the artist had seen. We have only to note the circumstance in which he changed the title *Moby Dick* to *Pasiphaë* to realize how little titles or even preliminary concepts had to do with the final painting. Lee Krasner Pollock recalls that upon completion of *Moby Dick,* James Johnson Sweeney was invited to see it: "The moment he walked in the door he said, 'that's Pasiphaë'." A lengthy discussion followed in which Sweeney told Pollock the story of Pasiphaë. It was Sweeney's poetic *interpretation* which convinced Pollock to change his title, as though he had read Pollock's unconscious intent more accurately than the artist.[25] Although Pollock may have adopted images from Surrealism which suggest ancient or mythological origins, mythology was clearly less important in the making of Pollock's art than in the naming of it. The painting, as though it indeed had "a life of its own," informed the artist of some profound personal truths which, in symbolic form, became his titles. In this regard, Mrs. Pollock recalls that once Jackson, referring to a painting in progress, asked her, "Is this a painting?" The question suggests that Pollock had so identified himself with the painting that he found it difficult to distinguish it from himself.

[25]It is surprising that O'Hara, aware of the painting's original title, could still write: "The stark, staring and foreboding figure of Pasiphaë is present, with her foreknowledge of the Minotaur and her lust...this is a recognition of the ritual which he is renewing. For in Pollock it is not a god in the form of a bull who seduces Pasiphaë—it is the bull." (*Jackson Pollock*, p. 19.)

Pollock's use of ancient models was less related to mythology than to his training under Benton and to the Jungian emphasis on the relevance of motifs produced out of impulses reflecting archetypes from the "collective unconscious." Benton had his students analyze reproductions of works of art from ancient Egypt and Assyria, as well as classical Greek, Roman and Renaissance works. But it would be absurd to suggest that Pollock's use of ritual, even of hieroglyphic motifs derived from an archeological awareness. Nor can it be said that such motifs reflect a literary interest in mythology. The sources of symbolism in Pollock's painting are much deeper, much more personal. His symbolism, as he himself says, originated in the unconscious, and its inspiration came not from myth but from a need to articulate his personal struggle.

It is sometimes suggested that the source of Pollock's drip style can be traced to his work in Siquieros' experimental workshop in 1936.[26] While Pollock may have been affected by that experience, a paint-splattered floor and experimentation with spray-guns is significantly different from his deliberate and controlled drip method of a decade later. He was doubtless also familiar with Hans Hofmann's experiments with drip painting, but even Hofmann did not see such techniques in the light of a formal method until after Pollock "pointed the way."[27] William Rubin's view of the intention of Pollock's drip method may apply to Hofmann more precisely than to Pollock; Hofmann's drip method developed out of a conscious, intellectual endeavor to "circumvent pictorial inhibitions" and traditional methods. It was, in that sense, conceptually nihilistic. Pollock's method, however, was not a denial of the image but a final and painful synthesis of image and action. While both artists arrived at a related solution to separate problems, this distinction between their individual motivations should be noted.

Further, by the time Pollock met Hofmann in 1942, the course of his development was already determined. That Pollock had already found his own direction is confirmed by his famous reply to Hofmann's suggestion that he should do more work from nature: "I am nature," meaning that he

[26]*Op. cit.* O'Connor, "The Genesis of Jackson Pollock," p. 21.

[27]Sam Hunter, "Jackson Pollock: The Maze and the Minotaur," *New World Writing,* New York: New American Library, 1956, p. 179.

acknowledged only one source of inspiration, only one authentic impulse —the one within.

A similar conviction of autonomy may have accounted for Pollock's refusal to participate in a Surrealist exhibition of psychic automatism, on the grounds that he did not like "group activity."[28] His art was, after all, linked to Surrealism only by a partly shared vocabulary developed in a continuous process of transcending the collective rhetoric of "schools" and dedicated to the creation of an autonomous esthetic.

In recent years, art historians have produced some excellent studies of the diverse influences which shaped Pollock's mature style. Chief among these is William Rubin's essay "Jackson Pollock and the Modern Tradition," which finds the Impressionists standing "midway . . . between the old masters and Pollock."[29] Yet Rubin's reassertion of a continuous evolution of style—from Impressionism to Pollock—merely labels events in a time-sequence and serves no purpose beyond assuring us that the metamorphosis of Western culture is an orderly process—an order which we confer upon it after the fact. Curiously, we find our orderly process in events which are usually conceived in defiance of it. Thus Pollock fits our history, our "tradition," not because his was the next logical step in the orderly process but because his creative decisions altered the course of it. Pollock's stylistic development was related to an established "tradition" only insofar as his education in a medium conditioned his use of it as a vehicle for personal expression; and that, after all, is what distinguishes the makers of history from the followers of history.

That artists are led to creative decisions by some combination of the existential condition of the world, the artistic climate in which they work, and their own psychological make-up is an elementary observation. But the complex interaction of these and other circumstances, and our inability to separate their relative spheres, obliges us to assume that the most important influences derive from models within the scope of art history (though not necessarily limited to them) and that these are modi-

---

[28]*Op. cit.* O'Connor, *Jackson Pollock,* p. 26.

[29]William Rubin, "Jackson Pollock and the Modern Tradition," *Artforum,* V, "Part I," No. 6, Feb. 1967, pp. 14-22; "Part II," No. 7, March 1967, pp. 28-37; "Part III," No. 8, April 1967, pp. 18-31; "Part IV," No. 9, May 1967, pp. 28-33.

fied according to the artist's personality, technical development and creative potentiality.

If, however, as in the case of Jackson Pollock, the artist abruptly creates a dramatically original style and significantly departs from his already established methods, we are justified in asking whether this departure was the logical outcome of a merely "artistic" proclivity, or whether some peculiar combination of events in another realm may have generated his new creation or at least have acted as a catalyst. Given an almost infinite choice of alternatives, the artist's decision to follow one direction rather than another—and by so doing to discover a new esthetic —may be determined by circumstances only incidentally related to art itself. His genius as an artist is not thereby diminished, but is expressed by his ability to recognize the possibilities inherent in such circumstances and to derive inspiration from them.

Pollock derived sufficient inspiration from his work with Henderson to begin a period of intense activity in 1940. A year later, his brother Sanford wrote:

> Jackson's art...will, I am convinced, come to great impor-
> tance...we are sure that if he is able to hold himself together
> his work will become of real significance. His painting is ab-
> stract, intense, evocative in quality.

By 1942 Pollock had painted, in O'Hara's words, "his first masterpiece, *Male and Female*," and in 1943 he produced at least two more major works, *Pasiphaë* and *Guardians of the Secret*. 1942 was also the year of his first one-man show. Two years later, Clement Greenberg asserted that Pollock was "the strongest painter of his generation and perhaps the greatest one since Miró...he is not afraid to look ugly..."[30]

Pollock's career was thus under way. Unfortunately his mental condition and his alcoholism remained essentially unchanged until late 1947 when, under the care of a general practitioner, he stopped drinking altogether. Through 1950 he remained sober and had gained enough emotional strength to sustain one of the most creative and productive periods

[30]*The Nation,* April 1945, p. 397.

in his life. Between 1948 and 1950 his art ripened and for the first and last time was devoid of covert imagery. But alcoholism was only symptomatic of the psychological difficulties which had beset him from childhood, not their cause, and in 1951 Pollock began drinking again. This must have been the most painful relapse since his breakdown in 1938, and just as his recovery in 1939-1940 was characterized and perhaps facilitated by the evocation of unconscious images, he turned once more to that process.

Thus it is no coincidence that his return to imagery should reflect ideas and motifs conceived a decade earlier, during his work with Henderson. Through the '40's, Pollock had veiled his images; now he elicited them in such works as *Black and White Painting* (1951), which recalls drawing no. 1 of this series in both subject and composition. Never before had he allowed such images open expression, except in private drawings and underpaintings.

Only during his "classical" drip period (1948-1950) was Pollock free of his need to elicit unconscious experiences, and only then was his psychological stability sufficient to suspend his alcoholism and permit him to approach the canvas analytically, without therapeutic directives.

By 1951 Pollock had come full-circle from Benton's classical figurative orientation, through a complete obscuration of imagery, to an explicit figuration of his own. With his return to imagery, Pollock epitomized his personal struggle in such paintings as *Portrait and a Dream* (1953), in which he clearly separates the two processes out of which his work had developed. The veil has been torn from the portrait (a self-portrait?); the double aspects of his art, the double aspects of his personality, the antagonists in his struggle for survival, were openly acknowledged. Their conflict was never resolved.

Pollock had accepted the challenge of his mind and had confronted it in the "arena" of art. Bryan Robertson understood this when he wrote:

> For Pollock to draw continually from his subconscious was
> not a denial of the artist's responsibility but an added and
> terrible burden, an increased and optimistic acceptance of
> the potentialities of painting as an expression of life. His last
> act of affirmation in painting, *Scent,* has tragic undertones

...the search was ended, the great gesture was made, and the exorcism was complete. The effort killed him.[31]

During the period when Pollock was working with Dr. Henderson, he produced very few paintings; this newly published body of drawings will therefore contribute considerably to our still growing understanding of his art. Further, it affords us an occasion to look outside the confines of art history alone, beyond stylistic analysis, and to consider another, an inward aspect of the metamorphosis of creative genius. Like Pollock himself, we lack the words in which to express the promptings of our unconscious; we have, thanks to Pollock, more than words alone.

[31]*Op. cit.* Robertson, p. 150.

The Plates

Plate 1. Gouache, 21½ x 15½ in. **33**

Plate 2. Colored pencil, crayon, 15 x 11 in.

Plate 3. Colored pencil, 15 x 11 in. **35**

36   Plate 4. Colored pencil, 15 x 10⅞ in.

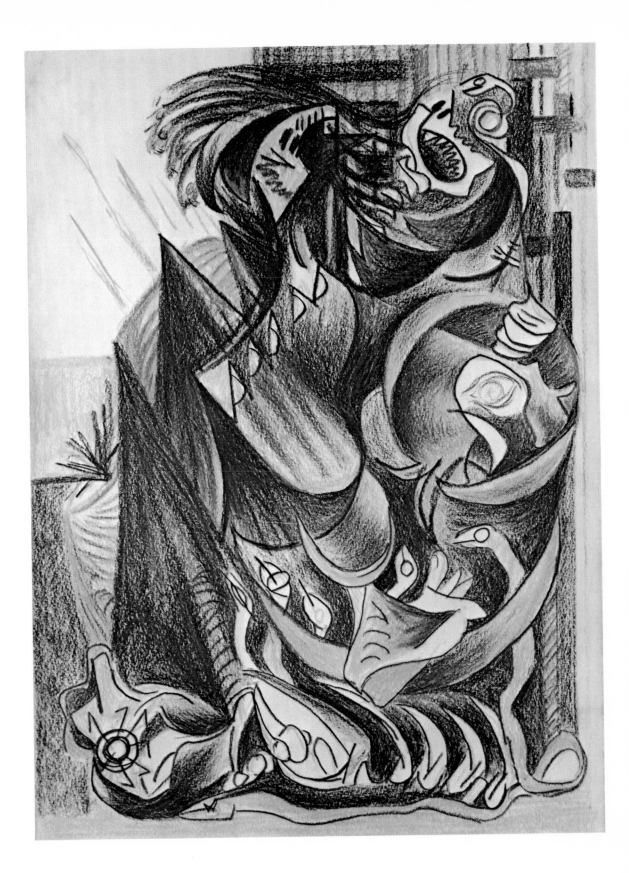

Plate 5. Colored pencil, 15 x 11 in.   **37**

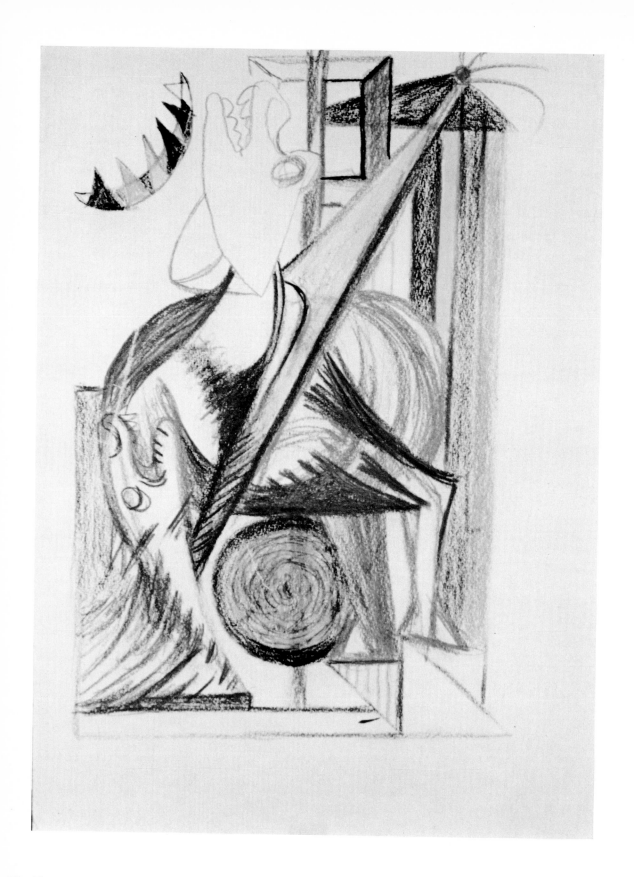

Plate 6. Colored pencil, 15 x 11 in.

Plate 7. Colored pencil, 10½ x 8¼ in. **39**

40   Plate 8. Colored pencil, lead pencil, 13 x 10¼ in.

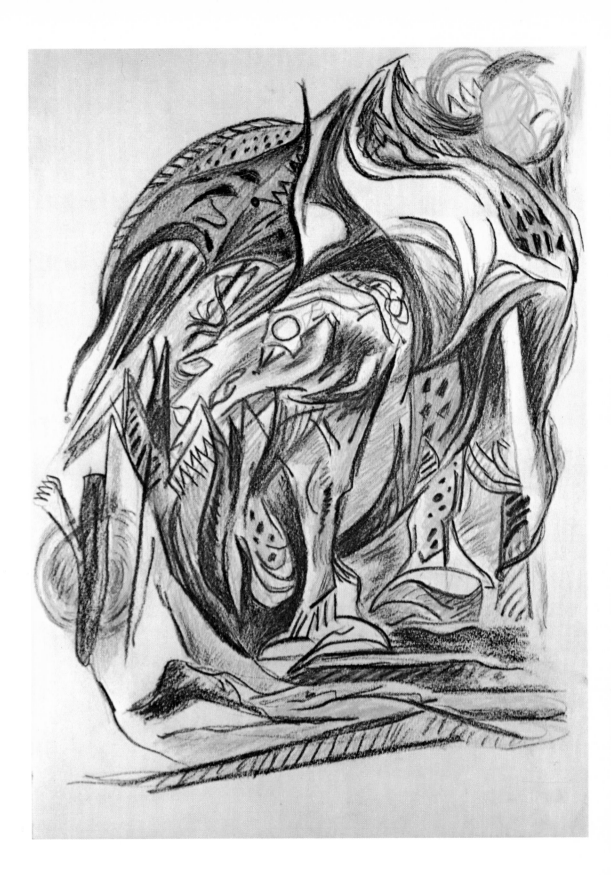

Plate 9. Colored pencil, 15 x 11 in. **41**

Plate 10. Colored pencil, ink, ink wash, 14 x 11 in.

Plate 11. Colored pencil, lead pencil, ink, ink wash, 14 x 11 in. **43**

44   Plate 12. Colored pencil, lead pencil, 6 x 6¾ in.

Plate 13. Colored pencil, lead pencil, 6 x 8¼ in. **45**

46   Plate 14 (reverse of 13). Colored pencil, lead pencil, 8¼ x 6 in.

Plate 15. Colored pencil, lead pencil, 6 x 7⅞ in.　**47**

48   Plate 16. Colored pencil, lead pencil, 6 x 7½ in.

50   Plate 18. Colored pencil, 15 x 10⅞ in.

Plate 19. Colored pencil, 9½ x 8¼ in. **51**

Plate 20. Colored pencil, 9¾ x 8¼ in.

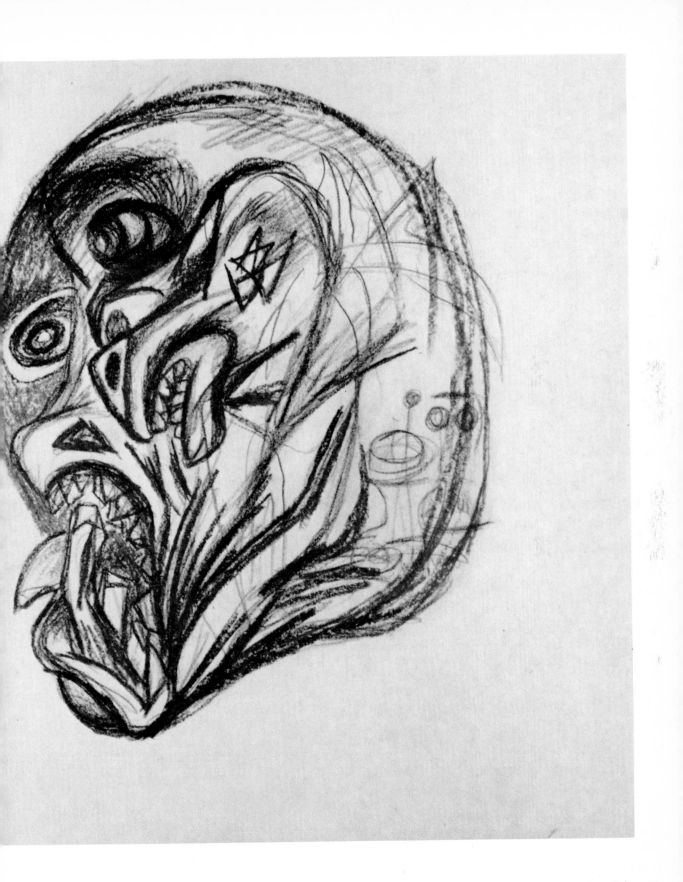

Plate 21. Colored pencil, lead pencil, 10¼ x 8¼ in. **53**

54 Plate 22. Colored pencil, 14 x 11 in.

Plate 23. Colored pencil, 10 x 8¼ in. **55**

Plate 24. Colored pencil, lead pencil, 14 x 11 in.

Plate 25. Colored pencil, lead pencil, 14 x 11 in. **57**

58 Plate 26. Colored pencil, 9¼ x 8¼ in.

Plate 27. Colored pencil, 15 x 11 in. **59**

Plate 28 (reverse of 27). Colored pencil, 15 x 11 in.

Plate 29. Colored pencil, 15 x 11 in. **61**

62 Plate 30. Colored pencil, lead pencil, 15 x 11 in.

Plate 31 (reverse of 30). Colored pencil, 15 x 11 in. **63**

Plate 32. Pencil, 15 x 11 in.

Plate 33 (reverse of 32). Colored pencil, 15 x 11 in. **65**

66 Plate 34. Colored pencil, lead pencil, 14 x 11 in.

Plate 35 (reverse of 34). Colored pencil, lead pencil, 14 x 11 in. **67**

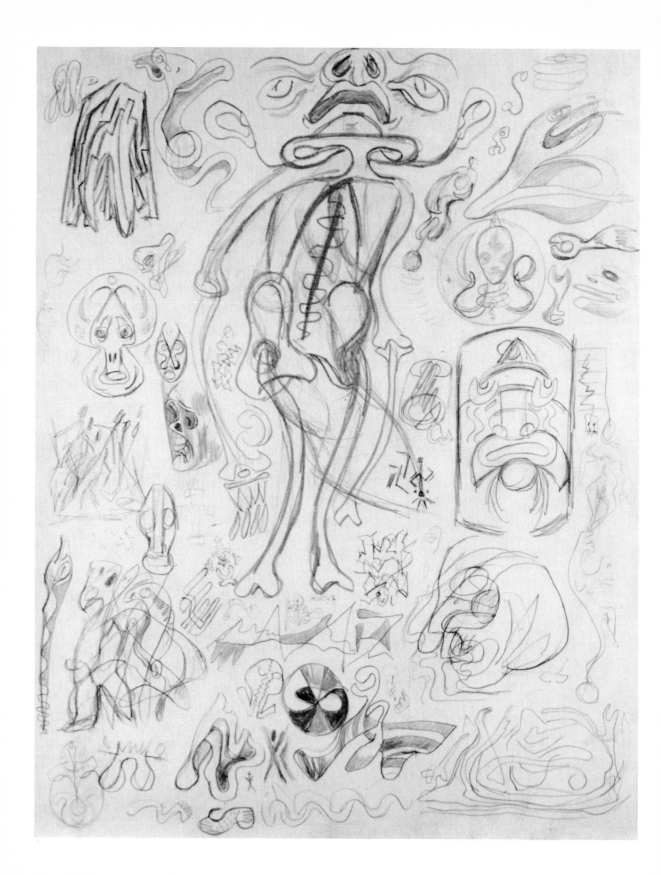

68   Plate 36. Colored pencil, lead pencil, 14 x 11 in.

Plate 37. Colored pencil, lead pencil, black ink, 14 x 11 in.   **69**

Plate 39 (reverse of 38). Pencil, 14 x 11 in. **71**

Plate 41 (reverse of 40). Colored pencil, 14 x 11 in. **73**

74   Plate 42. Colored pencil, lead pencil, 14 x 11 in.

Plate 43 (reverse of 42). Colored pencil, 14 x 11 in.   **75**

76   Plate 44. Colored pencil, 14 x 11 in.

Plate 45 (reverse of 44). Colored pencil, 14 x 11 in.   **77**

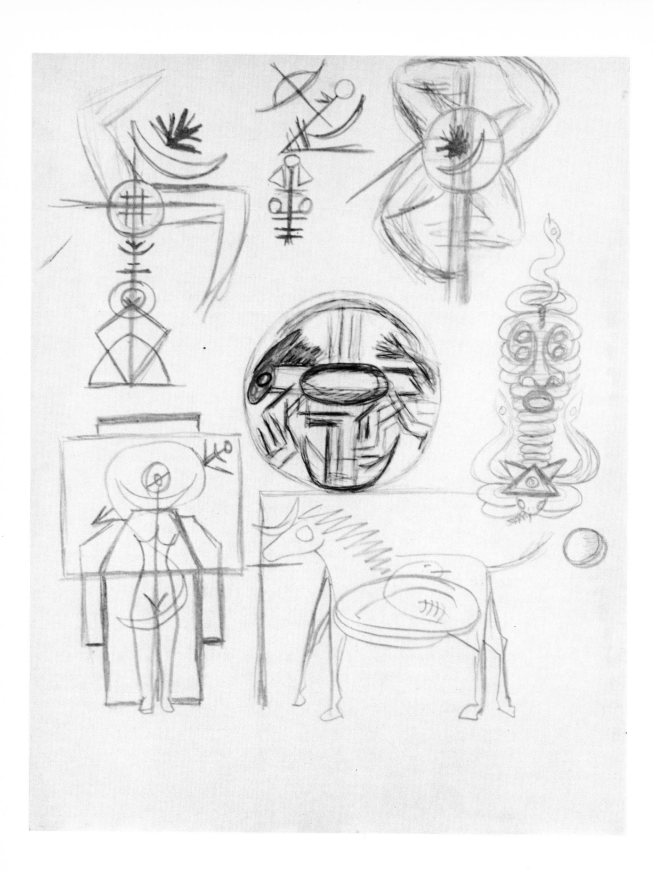

78   Plate 46. Colored pencil, lead pencil, 14 x 11 in.

Plate 47. Colored pencil, 15 x 11 in.   **79**

80   Plate 48 (reverse of 47). Colored pencil, 15 x 11 in.

Plate 49. Colored pencil, 15 x 11 in. **81**

82 Plate 50. Colored pencil, 15 x 11 in.

Plate 51 (reverse of 50). Colored pencil, 15 x 11 in.   **83**

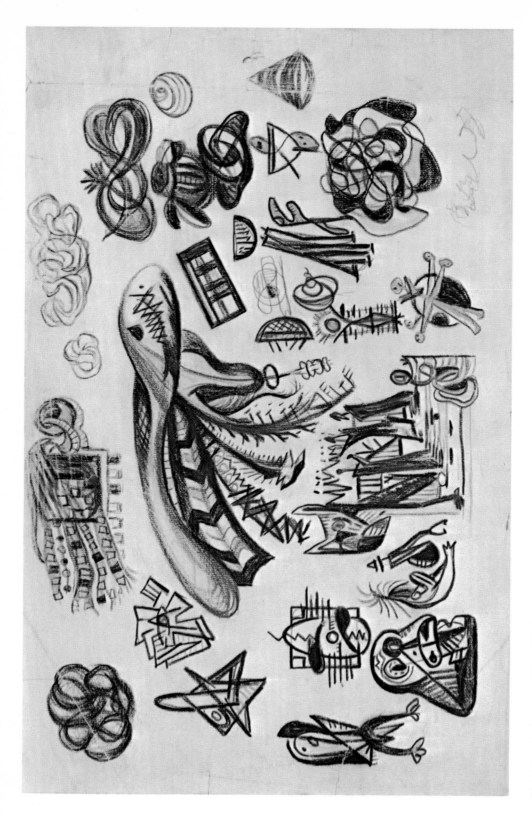

Plate 52. Pencil, crayon, 12⁵⁄₁₆ x 18⅜ in.

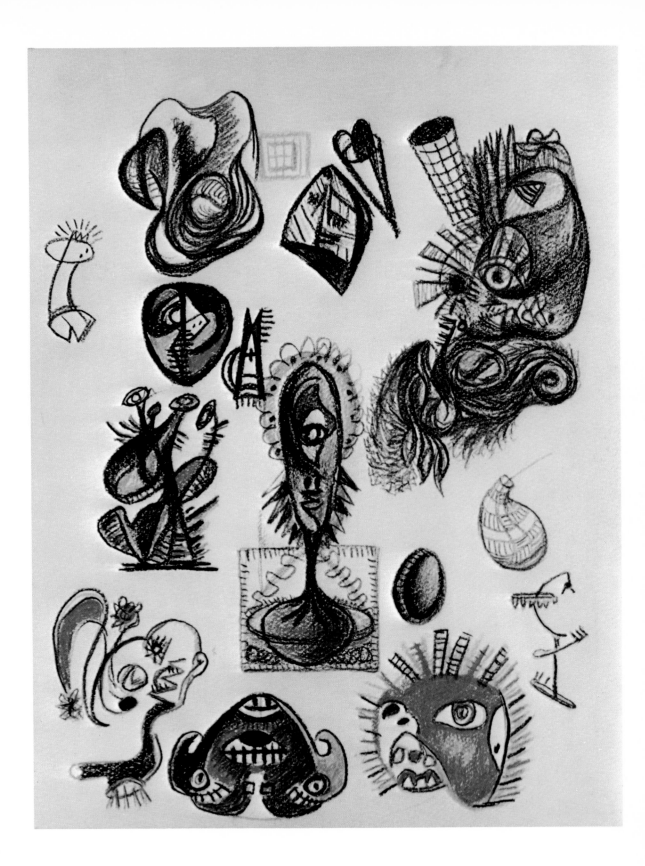

Plate 53. Colored pencil, lead pencil, 13 x 10¼ in.   **85**

Plate 54. Colored pencil, 15 x 11 in.

Plate 55 (reverse of 54). Colored pencil, 15 x 11 in.

Plate 56. Colored pencil, pencil, 12⅝ x 18½ in.

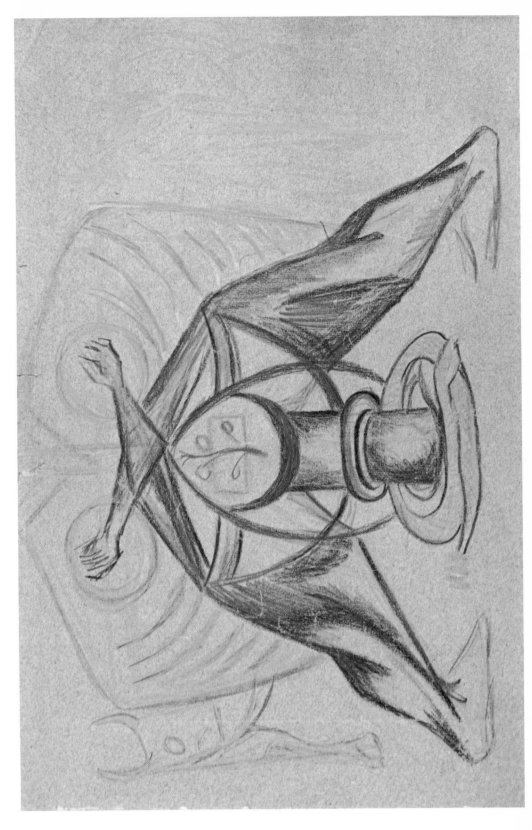

Plate 57. Colored pencil, crayon, 12¼ x 18¾ in.

90   Plate 58. Colored pencil, lead pencil, 9 x 8¼ in.

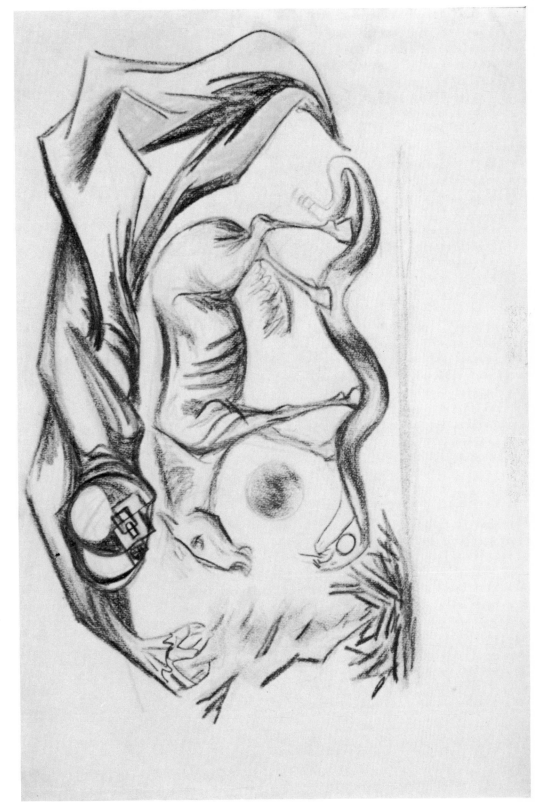

Plate 59. Colored pencil, 11⅞ x 18 in.

Plate 60. Colored pencil, 11⅞ x 17⅞ in.

Plate 61. Colored pencil, lead pencil, 11⅞ x 18 in.

Plate 62. Colored pencil, black ink, 6 x 4⅞ in.

Plate 63. Colored pencil, lead pencil, 5½ x 4 in.   **95**

Plate 64. Colored pencil, crayon, 12½ x 18⅝ in.

Plate 65. Colored pencil, lead pencil, 14 x 11 in.   **97**

Plate 66. Pencil, colored pencil, 15 x 11 in.

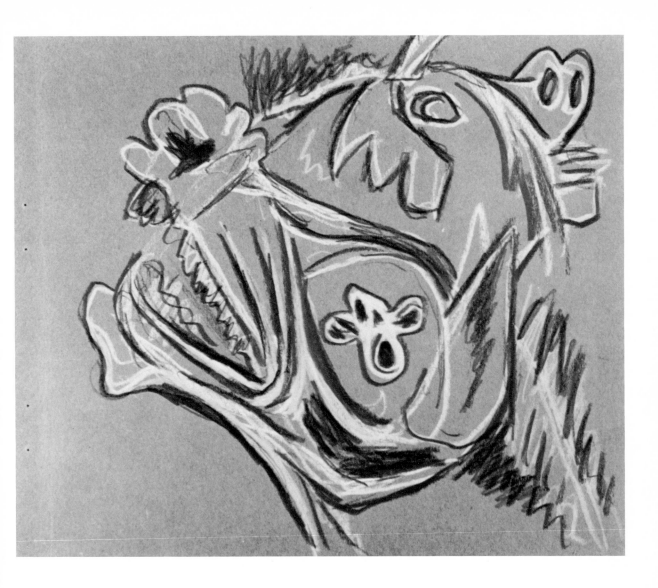

Plate 67. Colored pencil, lead pencil, 6 x 7⅛ in.   **99**

Plate 68. Colored pencil, lead pencil, 6 x 8¹¹⁄₁₆ in.

Plate 69. Colored pencil, crayon, 4 x 4 in., collection of Dr. & Mrs. Joseph Henderson **101**

Plate 70. Colored pencil, crayon, 5 x 5 in., collection of Dr. & Mrs. Joseph Henderson

Plate 71. Colored pencil, 7 x 4 in.   **103**

Plate 72. Colored pencil, 6⁹⁄₁₆ x 4 in.

Plate 73. Colored pencil, 6³⁄₁₆ x 4 in. **105**

106   Plate 74. Colored pencil, 6½ x 4 in.

Plate 75. Colored pencil, 4 x 6¹⁄₁₆ in.   **107**

108   Plate 76. Colored pencil, 6⅞ x 4 in.

Plate 77. Colored pencil, black ink, 5¼ x 6 in. **109**

110   Plate 78. Colored pencil, 8¹¹⁄₁₆ x 8¼ in.

Plate 79. Colored pencil, 8½ x 8¼ in. **111**

Plate 80. Colored pencil, 10 x 8¼ in.

Plate 81. Colored pencil, 8¼ x 7½ in. **113**

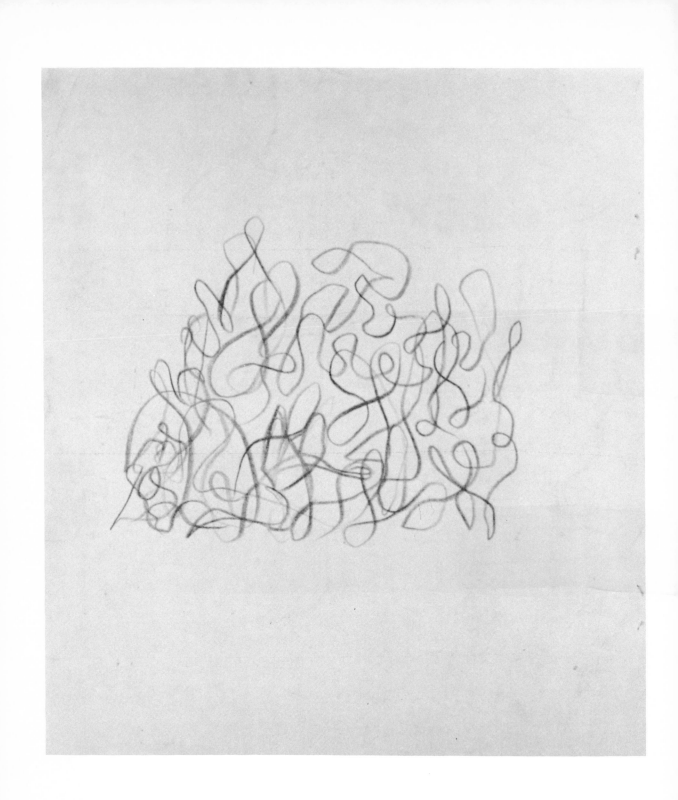

Plate 82 (reverse of 81). Colored pencil, 8¼ x 7½ in.

Plate 83. Colored pencil, lead pencil, 6 x 5¹¹⁄₁₆ in.   **115**

Bibliography

Alloway, Lawrence, "The Art of Jackson Pollock: 1912-1956," *Listener* (London), LX, November 27, 1958, p. 888.

_____, "The Biomorphic Forties," *Artforum,* Vol IV, No. 1, September 1965.

Ashton, Dore, *The Unknown Shore: A View of Contemporary Art.* Boston and Toronto: Little, Brown and Company, 1962.

Berger, John, 'The White Cell," *New Statesman,* LVI, November 22. 1958, pp. 722-23.

Ehrenzweig, Anton, *The Psycho-Analysis of Artistic Vision and Hearing.* New York: George Braziller, 1965.

Fried, Michael, "Jackson Pollock," *Artforum,* IV, September 1965, pp. 14-17.

Friedman, B. H., "Profile: Jackson Pollock," *Art in America,* XLIII, December 1955, pp. 49ff.

Glasner, Bruce, "Jackson Pollock. An Interview with Lee Krasner," *Arts Magazine,* XLI, April 1967, pp. 36-38.

Goodnough, Robert, "Pollock Paints a Picture," *Art News,* L, May 1951, pp. 38ff.

Greenberg, Clement, Reviews in *The Nation,* November 27, 1943, p. 621; April 7, 1945, p. 397; April 13, 1946, p. 445; December 28, 1946, p. 768; February 1, 1947, pp. 137, 139; January 24, 1948, p. 108; February 19, 1949, p. 221.

_____, "The Present Prospects of American Painting and Sculpture," *Horizon* (London), No. 93-94, October 1947, pp. 20-30.

_____, "Art Chronicle: Feeling Is All," *Partisan Review,* XIX, January-February 1952, p. 102.

_____, "Jackson Pollock's New Style," *Harper's Bazaar,* LXXXV, February 1952, p. 174.

_____, "'American-Type' Painting," *Partisan Review,* XXII, Spring 1955, pp. 186-87.

_____, "Jackson Pollock," *Evergreen Review,* I, 1957, pp. 95-96.

_____, "The Jackson Pollock Market Soars," *New York Times Magazine,* April 16, 1961, pp. 42ff.

_____, "America Takes the Lead, 1945-1965," *Art in America,* LIII, August-September 1965, p. 108.

———, "Jackson Pollock: 'Inspiration, Vision, Intuitive Decision,'" *Vogue,* CXLIX, April 1, 1967, pp. 160-61.

Hess, Thomas B., "Jackson Pollock 1912-1956," *Art News,* LV, September 1956, pp. 44-45.

Horn, Axel, "Jackson Pollock: The Hollow and the Bump," *Carleton Miscellany* (Northfield, Minn.), VII, Summer 1966, pp. 80-87.

Hunter, Sam, "Abstract Expressionism Then—and Now," *Canadian Art,* XXI, September/October 1964, pp. 266-68.

———, "Jackson Pollock: The Maze and the Minotaur," *New World Writing.* (Ninth Mentor Selection.) New York: New American Library, 1956.

Jung, C. G., and Kerenyi, C., *Essays on a Science of Mythology.* New York: Bollingen Series XXII, Pantheon Books, 1949.

Jung, Carl G., *Two Essays on Analytical Psychology.* Translated by R. F. C. Hull. New York: The World Publishing Co., 1956 (seventh printing, 1968).

Jung, Carl G., von Franz, M. L., Henderson, Joseph, *et. al., Man and His Symbols.* New York: Dell Publishing Company, 1964.

Kaprow, Allan. "The Legacy of Jackson Pollock," *Art News,* LVII, October 1958, pp. 24-26.

———, "Impurity," *Art News,* LXI, January 1963, pp. 53-54.

Kris, Ernst, *Psychoanalytic Explorations in Art.* New York: International Universities Press, 1952.

Lansford, Alonzo, "Automatic Pollock," *Art Digest,* XXII, January 15, 1948, p. 19.

Lavin, Irving, "Abstraction in Modern Painting: A Comparison," *Metropolitan Museum of Art Bulletin,* XIX, February 1961, pp. 166-71.

McClure, Michael, "Ode to Jackson Pollock," *Evergreen Review,* II, Autumn 1958, pp. 124-26.

O'Hara, Frank, *Jackson Pollock.* (The Great American Artists Series.) New York: George Braziller, 1959.

O'Connor, Francis V., "Growth Out of Need," *Report,* I, February 1964, pp. 27-28.

———, "The Genesis of Jackson Pollock: 1912 to 1943," *Artforum,* V, May 1967, pp. 16-23.

Phillips, William (ed.), *Art and Psychoanalysis.* New York: The World Publishing Co., 1963 (Copyright by Criterion books, 1957).

Read, Herbert, "The Limits of Painting," *Studio* (London), CLXVII, January 1964, pp. 3-4.

Robertson, Bryan, *Jackson Pollock.* New York: Harry N. Abrams, Inc., 1960.

Rose, Bernice, *Jackson Pollock: Works on Paper.* New York: The Museum of Modern Art, 1969.

Rubin, William, "Notes on Masson and Pollock," *Arts,* XXXIV, November 1959, pp. 36-43; December 1959, p. 9.

_____, "Jackson Pollock and the Modern Tradition," *Artforum,* V, February 1967, pp. 14-22; March 1967, pp. 28-37; April 1967, pp. 18-31; May 1967, pp. 28-33.

Tyler, Parker, "Jackson Pollock: The Infinite Labyrinth," *Magazine of Art,* XLIII, March 1950, pp. 92-93.

Valliere, James T. "The El Greco Influence on Jackson Pollock's Early Works," *Art Journal,* XXIV, Fall 1964, pp. 6-9.

"Jackson Pollock: An Artists' Symposium, Part I," *Art News,* LXVI, April 1967, pp. 29ff.; Part II, May 1967, pp. 27ff.

New York, The International Council at the Museum of Modern Art, *Jackson Pollock 1912-1956.* March 1, 1958-February 15, 1959.

New York, The Museum of Modern Art, *15 Americans.* April 9-July 27, 1953, 8 works by Pollock. Introduction by Alfonso Ossorio.

New York, The Museum of Modern Art, *Jackson Pollock.* December 19, 1956-February 3, 1957, p. 36. (The Museum of Modern Art Bulletin, XXIV, No. 2, 1956-57.

New York, Sidney Janis Gallery, *15 Years of Jackson Pollock.* November 28-December 31, 1955., p. 16.

ACKNOWLEDGMENTS

I am indebted in many ways to John I. H. Baur, Palmer French, B. H. Friedman, Thomas B. Hess, Richard Howard, Elizabeth Kennedy, Jerry Nordland, Charles Pollock, Lee Krasner Pollock, Wilma Stewart, Ruth Wysuph and especially Dr. Joseph Henderson and Fred Maxwell.

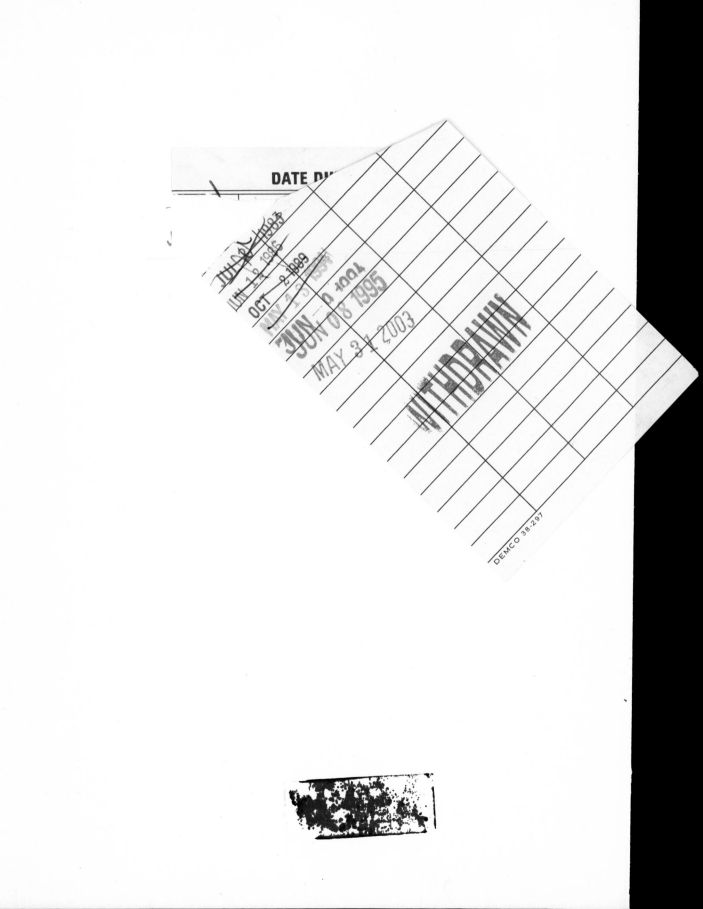